# Campbell Orr

## Pioneer of Association Football

### Football's Forgotten Founder

# Campbell Orr

## Pioneer of Association Football

---

**Douglas Gorman & Martin Shirley**

Martin Shirley
2017

First Printing: 2017

ISBN 978-1-5272-0472-0

www.CampbellOrr.com

# Contents

# Foreword

The game of Association Football, known by the majority of its hundreds of millions of followers worldwide simply as Football, can trace the origins of its current form back to the UK during the 1860s and 1870s. The game evolved rapidly during this period, until by the mid-1870s it had become what we, around 150 years later, would recognise as being very similar to the Football of today, played internationally in almost every country of the world.

But how was it that Association Football grew in popularity so fast in the late 1800s? The obvious answer is the enthusiasm of the early players, officials and clubs. Closer scrutiny, however, suggests that behind the scenes there were far-sighted individuals with in-depth knowledge of the game, hard at work establishing an outstanding organizational structure and unified Laws of the Game, which laid the foundations upon which the exceptional future success of Association Football was to be built.

Campbell Orr was my great grandfather, but beyond that I knew very little except that there was an unexplained family heirloom, a framed illuminated scroll which had passed from my grandfather to my mother and then to a dusty corner of my own home. The wording of the scroll suggested that Campbell Orr had been held in considerable esteem by his contemporaries in football, however over two generations of our family the significance of his involvement in the game had become almost entirely lost in the mists of time.

Douglas Gorman is a keen amateur football historian, and one of the frustrations which confront any historian, amateur or otherwise, is to discover what appears to be an untold nugget of history and then to be unable to unearth sufficient supporting information to take the story forward. This is the position in which Douglas found himself with regard to Campbell Orr, and there the story might have ended had not my aunt, Campbell Orr's granddaughter, reached the age of 90, when to celebrate her life we decided to compile an album of photographs and other memorabilia.

At this point the Campbell Orr story took a big leap forward, and missing pieces of a jigsaw which we hardly knew existed began to fall into place. Within my aunt's papers was a small file of newspaper cuttings and photographs which had been kept by my grandfather, mainly relating to his father Campbell Orr. Curiosity led to a brief internet search, that search led to an initial contact with Douglas Gorman, and Douglas rapidly realized the significance of the newspaper cuttings, photographs and illuminated scroll. His ongoing research has added many further pieces to the jigsaw, some of which have only recently come to light as ever more historical sources such as sports newspapers are digitised and made available via the internet.

This book tells the story, as we know it so far, of Campbell Orr. We are certain, however, that it is an unfinished story, with more information still likely to come to light from many sources. With this in mind, to accompany the publication of this book there is a website, www.CampbellOrr.com, through which we would request that anyone who knows further information or knows where further information might be found to please make contact with us, and on which we will present new and updated information as it becomes available. We will also provide links to sources through which to purchase the current edition of "Campbell Orr - Pioneer of Association Football", and in due course if sufficient additional information comes to light we will provide notifications with regard to any subsequent updated editions of the book.

Thank you on behalf of Douglas and myself for your interest, and please remember to visit www.CampbellOrr.com for our latest updates.

Martin Shirley
October 2017

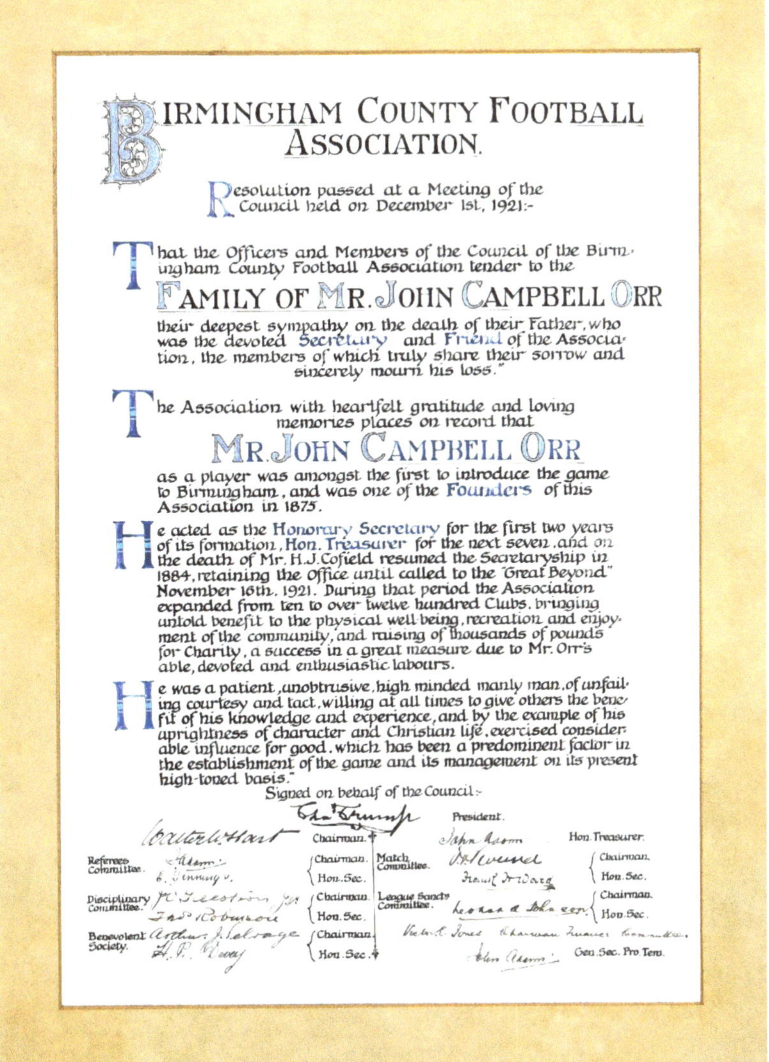

BIRMINGHAM COUNTY FOOTBALL ASSOCIATION.

Resolution passed at a Meeting of the Council held on December 1st, 1921:-

"That the Officers and Members of the Council of the Birmingham County Football Association tender to the

FAMILY OF MR. JOHN CAMPBELL ORR

their deepest sympathy on the death of their Father, who was the devoted Secretary and Friend of the Association, the members of which truly share their sorrow and sincerely mourn his loss."

"The Association with heartfelt gratitude and loving memories places on record that

MR. JOHN CAMPBELL ORR

as a player was amongst the first to introduce the game to Birmingham, and was one of the Founders of this Association in 1875.

He acted as the Honorary Secretary for the first two years of its formation, Hon. Treasurer for the next seven, and on the death of Mr. H.J. Cofield resumed the Secretaryship in 1884, retaining the office until called to the "Great Beyond" November 16th. 1921. During that period the Association expanded from ten to over twelve hundred Clubs, bringing untold benefit to the physical well being, recreation and enjoyment of the community, and raising of thousands of pounds for Charity, a success in a great measure due to Mr. Orr's able, devoted and enthusiastic labours.

He was a patient, unobtrusive, high minded manly man, of unfailing courtesy and tact, willing at all times to give others the benefit of his knowledge and experience, and by the example of his uprightness of character and Christian life, exercised considerable influence for good, which has been a predominent factor in the establishment of the game and its management on its present high-toned basis."

Signed on behalf of the Council:-

President.

Chairman. Hon. Treasurer.

Referees Committee. Chairman. Hon. Sec. Match Committee. Chairman. Hon. Sec.

Disciplinary Committee. Chairman. Hon. Sec. League Sanctions Committee. Chairman. Hon. Sec.

Benevolent Society. Chairman. Hon. Sec. Gen. Sec. Pro Tem.

**Illuminated scroll commemorating Campbell Orr**

An illuminated scroll of a resolution passed by the Council of the Birmingham County Football Association on 1 December 1921, signed by the Council members, framed and presented to the family of Campbell Orr.

For a full transcript of the text see Page 40.

# Introduction

John Campbell Orr, known by all as Campbell Orr, was a Scot who from 1872 devoted much of his adult life to Association Football, but who's pioneering role in the early years and the development of the Association game was barely recorded following his death in 1921 in his adopted home of Birmingham.

History can be fickle. The Glasgow Herald of 18 November 1921 simply recorded "***ORR*** *At Portend, City Road, Birmingham on 16th Inst. J Campbell Orr, son of the late John C Orr, Cupar Fife*". Meanwhile, however, in Birmingham his funeral was attended by a roll-call of Association Football names, and the Birmingham County Football Association presented his family with a framed signed illuminated scroll commemorating that he was a "*predominant factor in the establishment of the game and its management*". At the same time the Birmingham Sports Argus wrote that "*Without in any way appearing to belittle the work and worth [of others], the loss of Campbell Orr will affect the football world most*".

So how could history have overlooked the pioneering work of Campbell Orr, with barely a single photograph publically available? The answer would appear to be the simple matter of timing. Historians would have had many more important subjects on their minds in 1921, with The Great War having so recently ended. His obituaries were almost exclusively in local Birmingham newspapers, and might have been lost entirely had not one of Campbell Orr's sons cut them out to keep with several photographs, which together with the illuminated scroll ended up languishing in the homes of family members. Then in late 2013 Douglas Gorman's interest as a football historian in the almost unknown Campbell Orr very luckily coincided with preparations for the 90th birthday of one of Campbell Orr's granddaughters, at which time Martin Shirley, a great grandson of Campbell Orr, located Douglas via an internet search.

As a result of this collaboration and after over 90 years in obscurity the pioneering contribution of Campbell Orr to the establishment of Association Football can be recorded.

# Chapter 1: *"Grand Old Man of Midlands football"*

The *"Grand Old Men of Midlands football"* was the description often given to William McGregor (founder of the Football League), Charles Crump (Senior Vice President of the Football Association and President of the Birmingham County Football Association), Edward Moss Mitton (footballer, referee, cricketer and preacher who saw the social benefits of the game) and Campbell Orr (footballer, referee, journalist and Secretary of the Birmingham County Football Association).

The Birmingham Sports Argus, in a tribute to Campbell Orr on 19 November 1921, reflected on the loss of McGregor, Mitton and now Campbell Orr saying: *"Without in any way appearing to belittle the work and worth of either William McGregor or Edward Moss Mitton, the loss of Campbell Orr will affect the football world most"*. The writer, a close associate of all three men writing under the pseudonym *"Argus Junior"*, saw fit to describe Campbell Orr as *"the greatest of all football pioneers."*

This is the story of Campbell Orr, who until 1870 seemed destined for success on the Rugby field. But for a change in his family fortunes we may have been writing about one of the Scots in the very first Rugby International in 1871. Instead the story is of the Scot who, together with a fellow Scot, brought Association Football to the city of Birmingham and formed the city's first club, and who went on to play a leading role in the organisation, development and administration of the Association game in its early and formative years.

**Campbell Orr circa 1910 - 1920 The "*Grand Old Man of Midlands football*"**

# Chapter 2: Born and raised in Scotland

John Campbell Orr, known as Campbell Orr, was born in Glasgow on 21 October 1850. He was the son of John Cunningham Orr, born in Maybole, Ayrshire, and Wilhelmina Campbell, born in Glyde, County Louth, Ireland. Wilhelmina was the daughter of John Campbell and Jane Brackenridge. Her wealthy uncle, Gavin Brackenridge, is said to have given her a finishing education in Liverpool, and she and John Cunningham Orr are said to have met in Maybole, Ayrshire.

Shortly after Campbell Orr's birth the family moved to Cupar in Fife, where John C Orr worked as a bookkeeper and cashier for a local firm. In 1857 John C Orr went into partnership with a Mr Whitehead in a stationery, printing and publishing business. This included publication of the Fife Herald, a newspaper originally started by the well-known Tullis printing family, which is still in existence and published by Johnston Press plc. However, the partnership with Mr Whitehead was dissolved acrimoniously in November 1858, and many years of financial pressure eventually led to the bankruptcy of the business. In the Edinburgh Gazette of 16 April 1869 a notice was published announcing the sequestration of John C Orr's estate for the benefit of his creditors.

There can be little doubt that his father's business troubles were to alter the direction of Campbell Orr's entire adult life, not least with regard to his sporting career.

# Chapter 3: Rugby at the University of St Andrews

Campbell Orr was educated at Abbey Park School, St Andrews and the University of St Andrews. He enrolled at St Andrews in 1868 aged 18, and in his first year he read English Literature and Mathematics. During his second year he studied Logic, Mathematics and Physiology & Hygiene.

William McGregor, another Scot and "*Grand old man of Midlands football*", later used the term "*The Rugbyite*" in describing his friend Campbell Orr's early interest in Rugby Football. Rugby Football was played at the University of St Andrews and Campbell Orr was a good player, a regular member and captain-elect of the University team. Had he not left the university before his third year, his progression in the world of Rugby could have been significant. He said later "*Perhaps I may without self-gratification say that I was unlucky not to get my international [Rugby] cap for Scotland.*"

He could indeed have been capped at Rugby. The last record of him playing Rugby Football was on Saturday 5 February 1870 for the University of St Andrews against Edinburgh Academical at Raeburn Place, Edinburgh. In the match report he was described as being "*particularly active*". Just over a year later six of the players in that game represented Scotland in the first Rugby International versus England at the same ground. The Scotland team included the St Andrews captain, Robert Munro, who Campbell Orr had been due to replace in the next season. Also in the team was a former schoolmate from Abbey Park School, JLH MacFarlane (Edinburgh University).

# Chapter 4: *"The Rugbyite"* moves to Birmingham

It is a reasonable assumption that the collapse of his father's business disrupted Campbell Orr's university education, particularly its funding. It is recorded that in 1870 Campbell Orr was the recipient of the Cupar Bursary, a presentation bursary awarded by Cupar Town Council. It is also recorded that *"Provost Hood [the convenor of Cupar Town Council] thought they could not do better than to bestow the bursary on Mr Orr; he understood he was a man of great promise. This was unanimously agreed to."* However, Campbell Orr's university education appears to have ended after two years, and with it ended two years of significant achievements on the Rugby field and the prospect of playing Rugby for his country.

In the 1871 Census (2 April 1871) Campbell Orr was in Edinburgh and was a *"Clerk to Writer to Signet"* (a clerk to a solicitor). Then in 1872 he chose to move to Birmingham, joined the Clerks' Association and pursued a career as a merchant's clerk.

In a coincidence of timing which was to change the direction of his sporting career, Campbell Orr moved to Birmingham at about the same time as several other Scots whose sporting interest lay in Association Football. These Scots, together with others, were to be at the forefront of the rapid growth of Association Football in the following years.

Campbell Orr the successful Rugby footballer was soon to become Campbell Orr the pioneer of Association Football.

**Campbell Orr in his early twenties, shortly after his arrival in Birmingham in 1872**

# Chapter 5: Calthorpe Football Club of Birmingham

Founded in 1873 by Campbell Orr and John Carson, initially as the Birmingham Clerks' Football Club, Calthorpe Football Club was the first Association Football club in Birmingham. The Birmingham Clerks' Association, to which both men belonged, was the association of articled clerks from the commercial and legal world in the city.

There is good historical evidence that not only was the Birmingham Clerks' Football Club the first Association Football club in Birmingham, but also that it was the first by several months or perhaps as much as a year. Campbell Orr is on record as saying that he and John Carson, a fellow Scot who had been a member of Queen's Park Football Club in Glasgow, introduced the game of Association Football to Birmingham. If someone challenged that assertion he would say *"for a time the Birmingham Clerks' Football Club, as we called ourselves, could find no opponents here."* In the very early days games were played among club members for the want of opponents. He would also point out that while Association Football was being played in the nearby Black Country (the industrial West Midlands) it was not being played in the city of Birmingham. The Birmingham Daily Post of 15 October 1886 wrote that *"the Calthorpe club under the tutorship of Mr Carson and Mr Orr commenced to play the Association game in 1873, and the Birmingham Association began its useful career of admirable management in 1875."*

The first question for the Birmingham Clerks' Football Club was to decide which code of play to adopt. Campbell Orr had only played Rugby Football while John Carson had only played the Association Football game. Campbell Orr's rugby prowess at St Andrews was well known. John Carson was an accomplished Association player, scoring a goal for Queen's Park in a 14-a-side game against Airdrie Football Club on 23 June 1870 under the London Association Rules (Queen's Park won 4-0).

John Carson would not hear of the Rugby code. On the other hand, Campbell Orr believed that any footballer could adapt to play either Association or Rugby football. In 1902, talking about the early days of the game in Birmingham, William McGregor, the founder of the Football League, said that *"If it had rested with Mr Orr the Birmingham Clerks' Football Club would have adopted the Rugby rules"*. McGregor went on to say *"Mr Carson, however, had never played Rugby and as it is easier for a Rugby player to adapt himself to the Association code than for an Association expert to develop ability in the other game, Association was decided upon, Mr Carson being very strong on this score. He had no difficulty in carrying his point, as the other members were by no means keen as to how the matter went."*

John Carson obtained a copy of the rules from his former club, Queen's Park FC. With a few modifications these rules were adopted by the Birmingham Clerks' FC. Their first match was against a club referred to as *"the Shakespeare"* on 9 March 1873. In the search for games they played against Moseley Rugby Football Club where one half was played under the Rugby code and the other under the Association code. Matches played at Wednesbury were a particular challenge where the Wednesbury club rules needed to be adopted by the Birmingham visitors. Campbell Orr would, many years later, recall that *"in a game at Wednesbury touches behind the goal were allowed for which they got a free kick from a corner. The game was not a success from a football point of view, and they resolved there and then that they would never have any more touchdowns"*.

The games played under mixed rules, known as *"medley games"*, were played as late as 1874, and by all accounts Campbell Orr's all-round footballing skills came to the fore. William McGregor said of his friend's participation: *"It is imagined this style of play suited him to a nicety. He was not only an excellent Association forward but an expert at the Rugby style and he used to secure these tries with avidity. In obtaining one try at Wednesbury he ran clean into the wire fence on the boundary."*

William McGregor had arrived in Birmingham from Perthshire two years before Campbell Orr. They had met when the Calthorpe club was founded. McGregor, whose draper's shop was in the Aston district of the city, then joined the new Aston Villa Football Club. The two remained friends and their paths would cross many times in football affairs.

Calthorpe FC was unable to develop as other teams in the city did, because it was a tenant of the tightly regulated Calthorpe Estate and was unable to charge an entry fee to spectators to help finance the running costs. It is probable that the club was able to carry on longer than expected due to the financial support from its members. Calthorpe FC continued in existence but at a lower level until around 1928, but it is understood that in his later years Campbell Orr had a connection with Small Heath Alliance (today's Birmingham City FC).

Had Calthorpe FC been able to develop more rapidly in the early years then its future could have been very different. The story is often told of how Archie Hunter, arriving from Scotland in Birmingham, tried to find the Calthorpe club which he had played against for Ayr Thistle during the first-ever tour by a Birmingham club. He was unable to find where Calthorpe played but came across and watched a cricket match instead. However, he ended up joining the recently formed Aston Villa Football Club. Archie Hunter's work colleague George Uzell encouraged him to join *"The Villa"*, but he was uncertain until he heard that fellow Scot George Ramsay was captain of the club. Archie Hunter went on to be the first Villa captain to lift the FA Cup in 1886/87.

It is notable that, following the decision to adopt Association Football rules at the Calthorpe club, Campbell Orr subsequently became a leading advocate of the safer Association code, which he would later contrast with the "*rough and dangerous*" aspects of the Rugby code.

# Chapter 6: Calthorpe FC versus Queen's Park FC (Glasgow)

The combination of Campbell Orr's foresight together with John Carson's connections resulted in the organisation of a match against the second team of Queen's Park Football Club. The famous Glasgow club was formed in 1867, with a second eleven team being established in 1871. This team was known as the Second Queen's Park and did not adopt their more familiar name, the Strollers, until 1885.

Campbell Orr played for Calthorpe in the first game against the Second Queen's Park on Saturday 3 February 1877 on Calthorpe's ground at Bristol Road, Birmingham. The Birmingham Daily Gazette reported a 4-3 win for the visitors but centre forward J C Orr scored the first Calthorpe goal and had a part in the second.

Later that year on 8 December 1877 the Second Queen's Park FC visited Birmingham again to play Calthorpe and had an 8-0 victory. Campbell Orr and John Carson would have been delighted to have secured and played in a fixture against a team from what was probably the strongest club in the United Kingdom at that time.

# Chapter 7: Retirement as a player

After hanging up his boots in his early thirties around 1882/83, Campbell Orr regularly officiated at games and represented the Calthorpe club in an official capacity, even when his other commitments meant that he had to reduce his football administrative work for a short time. He was later involved in the examination of new referees.

He officiated at Birmingham Football Association Cup matches and was one of two umpires in a semi-final tie at Aston Lower Grounds, today's Villa Park, between Walsall Swifts and Wednesbury Old Athletic on 24 March 1883. Until 1891 matches were controlled by two umpires, with a referee in charge of time-keeping and ruling when the umpires could not agree. When, in 1891, the Football Association proposed the change to a referee and two linesmen it was Campbell Orr's friend, Charles Crump, who attended the meeting of the International Football Association Board that made the decision. The establishment and role of the Board is explained in Chapter 10, Development of the game.

He made contributions titled *"Football Notes"* to the *"Midland Athlete"*, a weekly sports newspaper, under the pen name *"Don Juan"*, and was the first such commentator of the game in Birmingham. This started because of the need of emerging clubs to provide their own match reports to the newspapers of the day.

Campbell Orr published the first football annual in Birmingham in October 1882. Titled *"The Midland Football Annual"*, it contained a comprehensive review of the 1881/82 season. The Birmingham Daily Post described it as *"embracing almost everything that can be given to the public in connection with football"*. Although it was only published for one year it paved the way for a later annual publication the *"Midland Athletic Star – Football Record – Birmingham and District"* and other similar publications that continue to the present day.

John Carson on the other hand appears to have played no further part in Association Football after around 1883, although he continued to live in Small Heath, Birmingham, and his sport

## THE OLD BRIGADE.

This picture shows some members of famous local teams 50 years ago. They are believed to have been assembled as representing the Birmingham and District F.A. The names are (left to right): Back row: J. Campbell Orr (hon. treasurer), W. B. Mason (vice-president), H. Evans (Derby Midland), Jos. Arnall (vice-president), J. H. Cofield (hon. secretary), Chas. Crump (president). Middle row: G. H. Holden (Wednesbury Old Athletic), A. James (Small Heath Alliance), T. Bryan (Aston Villa) (captain), A. Harvey (Aston Villa), H. Vaughton (Aston Villa), W. Yates (Walsall Swifts). Front row: S. Law (Aston Villa), A. Brown (Aston Villa), Eli Davis (Aston Villa).

**"The Old Brigade"**

**The players and officials who represented the Birmingham and District FA in 1881/82**

Campbell Orr is standing at top left and Charles (Chas) Crump is seated at far right, in a dark suit.

Birmingham won two matches played at Aston Lower Grounds, against Sheffield on 26 December 1881 (result 2:1) and against the Scottish Counties on 25 February 1882 (result 3:1). Newspaper cutting source unknown was now as a keen bowler and a member of the Yardley Arms Bowling Club. He moved upon retirement to Lyme Regis where he lived until his death in 1931. His obituary said that *"he could rarely be tempted into reminiscence."* However, John Carson left his mark on the club in another way: in his book "*Lost teams of the Midlands*" Mike Bradbury's extensive research reveals that Calthorpe played in the same black and white hoops as had John Carson's former club Queen's Park FC.

# Chapter 8: Secretary of Birmingham County Football Association

The Birmingham District and Counties Football Association was formed in 1875, and Campbell Orr was its first Honorary Secretary. He held office for two years before his work as a football journalist forced him to stand down, at which time he took the office of Honorary Treasurer. In 1886 following Joseph "Joe" Cofield's death, Campbell Orr, persuaded in part by William McGregor, stepped up to become Secretary once again. He continued in this role for 35 years until his own death in 1921, by which time the Birmingham FA had over 1,200 affiliated clubs.

Whilst researching this book, it has become apparent to the authors that, although Campbell Orr's primary official position was with the Birmingham Association, he was an influential and leading figure in the early development of the Laws and the organisational structure of Association Football. He played a significant part in remodelling the constitution of the initial London-based Football Association so that it encompassed the needs of the County Associations nationwide. These developments laid the organisational foundations for the rapid growth of Association Football across England and the other home nations. These topics will be covered in more detail in later chapters.

At the national level within English football, Campbell Orr was County Representative for Birmingham, and is understood to have served on the Council of the Football Association for around 25 years. He was an influential figure at the annual meeting of the secretaries of all the County Football Associations, including Scottish, Welsh and Irish representatives. The outcome of these meetings was the fixture list for the coming season for internationals and other representative matches, and the dates for the rounds of the various knock-out cup competitions. For many years, along with Tom Hindle of Darwen Football Club, he was joint auditor of the Football Association accounts. It is likely, however, that it was as a member of the Council that he made his most significant contributions to the development of the game.

Campbell Orr was very active in publicising the developments in the game. In his capacity as Secretary he entered a long-running correspondence through the Letters to the Editor of the Daily Post on the differences between Rugby and Association Football, including what he saw as the important topic of the safety of the players. In a letter covering this subject dated 23 March 1876 he pointed out that *"all the rough and dangerous principles of the Rugby code are carefully excluded"* and helpfully enclosed a copy of the game's new rules for the editor's perusal. He pointed out that the Calthorpe club had been playing almost weekly matches for three years *"and not a single member has been even slightly hurt."*

Alongside his work on developing the organisation of the game at the County and National level, he dealt with local disputes and disciplinary matters that are all part of any football administrator's workload. The newspapers of the day regularly mention Campbell Orr dealing with disputes between clubs and the eligibility of players. Apart from his knowledge of the rules, he was seen as a fair dealer and his opinion was sought out by local leagues on a range of topics. In 1918 he oversaw changes to the rules and constitution of the Birmingham FA to give the junior clubs more representation on the council, and to bring hitherto unaffiliated local leagues into the Birmingham FA fold. This was a thorny issue that took up most of 1918 to resolve.

Campbell Orr was also involved in organising competitions and matches to raise funds for charity. During the First World War it was agreed that football should not be played for profit and as a consequence net gate receipts should be paid to charity. This responsibility fell to Campbell Orr, who needed all his diplomacy skills to ensure the correct amounts were collected from the semi-professional leagues who appeared more reluctant than the amateur clubs and leagues to make the correct contributions. During this time he also worked with the Voluntary Recruiting League to encourage football clubs to do all they could to ensure that their players joined the armed forces. Three of his own sons served during the war. His friend Edward Moss Mitton also worked tirelessly during the war years to maintain football and use it to raise funds for forces charities. This other *"Grand Old Man of Midlands football"* was also a supporter of the junior clubs and competitions, and a founder of the Birmingham Works FA and Birmingham Wednesday FA. During the War he arranged charity

**Campbell Orr, in middle age, date unknown**

matches, often organising his own *"Mr E M Mitton's XI"* and playing in goal, ensuring that competitive football continued for those boys below military age.

Campbell Orr was a man who was willing to express opinions and who was listened to. For example, in April 1898 he wrote to the newspapers about what he saw as the unjustified criticism heaped on his fellow Birmingham-based Scot James Cowan of Aston Villa. He took the Scottish Football Association and Scottish press to task over their negative assessment of Cowan's performance for Scotland against England in the international. There had been doubts about Cowan's fitness before the game and doubts afterwards as to whether he had been entirely truthful on that score with the selectors. He became the scapegoat for the Scottish defeat. Campbell Orr noted that *"his play was not so successful nor so brilliant as usual, but he was by no means a failure, and there were many worse players on the field on Saturday"*. In his opinion Cowan had been justified in playing *"an individual, selfish game because he had no support; but apart from this he was the best man on the Scottish side"*. He also pointed out the quality of the opposition - *"the brilliant eleven that represented England"*.

Footnote: The title *"Honorary Secretary"* at that time did not mean non-executive or voluntary as the term would more commonly imply today. It is recorded that in 1886 Campbell Orr received an annual salary of 50 Guineas (£52.50), which would have supplemented his salary as a merchant's clerk.

# Chapter 9: Development of the game

Following the formation of the Birmingham District and Counties Football Association in 1875, the game developed rapidly in the Birmingham area. Within just two years over a dozen clubs had been established, and the Birmingham Association, with Campbell Orr as its Honorary Secretary, took a lead as it swiftly codified the laws under which its clubs played and set about organising the game.

These first three years, 1875 to 1877, were crucial in the development of Association Football both locally and nationally, and Campbell Orr played a significant part. When he took office in 1875 the laws of the game were not as they are today. The Sheffield Rules were widely used in the North of England between 1857 and 1877. Meanwhile an adapted version of the Cambridge Rules were adopted by the London-based fledgling Football Association on its formation in 1863 for use by its founding London-based clubs. Campbell Orr ensured that the Birmingham Association adopted these Football Association rules as they stood at that time. Then as Secretary he established the influence of the new Birmingham-based Association in the nation-wide discussions and negotiations to bring into force a single set of laws in 1877. For example, Birmingham acted as the mediators to resolve the different views on the offside law, over which Sheffield eventually conceded to London.

This success in establishing a single version of the Laws of the Game led to a significant increase in the number of clubs competing in the FA Challenge Cup Competition, and this in turn paved the way for the formation of the Football League in 1888. Wednesbury Strollers were the first West Midlands club to enter the FA Challenge Cup in 1878/79, followed by a team called Birmingham (unconnected to today's Birmingham City) in 1879/80. In 1880/81 Calthorpe and Aston Villa entered.

Laws of the Game were agreed by the four Home Nations Football Associations in 1882 and led to the first international competition in 1884. Responsibility for the Laws was vested in the International Football Association Board in 1886, at that time consisting of England, Scotland, Ireland and Wales, which in turn provided the basis for global growth of the game.

The International Board retains that responsibility today, with the founding nations having 50% of the votes and FIFA having the other 50%.

# Chapter 10: Campbell Orr on rules and organisation

On Thursday 28 September 1893 Campbell Orr gave a wide-ranging speech on Association Football to the Midland Daily Telegraph Association. The Association organised the Midland Daily Telegraph Association Football Cup, the leading competition for junior clubs. The speech covered the history of the game and current developments, and a newspaper report of the speech in the Midland Daily Telegraph of 30 September 1893 ran to several thousand words.

Given that there is considerable evidence that Campbell Orr was at the very heart of the early development of the game, the parts of his speech which refer to the development of the rules and organisational structure of the Football Association merit being quoted in full. It is reasonable to speculate that the journalist who wrote the lengthy report was either very good at shorthand, or more likely was given sight of the prepared speech. Furthermore, as Campbell Orr was by all accounts modest and not given to self-aggrandisement, the speech is likely to be an accurate record of events. The press report can, therefore, be regarded as virtually a first-hand historical summary of the initial years of the organisational development of the Football Association.

The following paragraphs are quoted verbatim from the press report, with only minimal editing for clarity which is identified in square brackets. It is easy to envisage Campbell Orr speaking the words himself at the time, with of course "I" replacing "He" as written by the reporter. Despite being given over 120 years ago, the speech is as understandable today as it would have been in 1893:

"He had not required to study his subject, or to turn up any treatise upon football before he came there, to explain the rules of Association football. He could explain the rules of the game without doing that, seeing that all through the football life of Birmingham and district he had been, he might say, at the helm. He had had something to do with the alteration or proposal of every rule that they had played under".

"The new order of football began about 1863, or more recently than that, when some enthusiast in London conceived the idea of harmonising the various football rules in the country, known as the Association rules. An association was then formed, and from that body sprang the present [Football] Association, without there being, practically, any break. About the year he had mentioned the Association game was played very similar to the Rugby game of to-day, and among other things they had three touches behind the goal line. But what were considered objectionable features were at length eliminated, and about the year 1871 the association revised the rules, stopped all handling of the ball, and established what was now known as Association football".

"In the year [1873] he had the honour of founding the first association football club in Birmingham. They played about two matches that year amongst themselves, as there were no other clubs for them to play with. The next year they had one or two clubs around them. The rules then were very conflicting, and the captains of teams before a match always held consultations as to what points should be allowed, and what points should not be allowed". "Two years later the Birmingham Football Association was founded. They started with 10 clubs, and the second year had 15".

"At the time he had referred to [1873] football was governed from London and Sheffield, and there was naturally a cross between the rules of the two towns. This was over the offside rule, which Sheffield would not recognise. The Birmingham Association tried to be the medium of uniting the two sections, and eventually Sheffield gave way. Then it was the practice that when the ball went into goal to butt at the goal-keeper as hard as one could. But when they obtained unanimity on that point they found that Scotland was against them. In the course of time, however, that opposition was overcome, and for many years past England, Scotland, Ireland, and Wales had worked in co-operation with each other, and football was now governed by arbitration – by an international board composed of representatives of the four countries".

"But there was something more to be done. The followers of the game in Birmingham felt that it was not just the thing to be ruled and governed by a few gentlemen in London who did not represent them, and to some extent did not represent their views and their feelings. They wanted to alter that. It took a long time to do it, but gradually they got representatives [to] London from Lancashire, Sheffield, and other districts, and the result was that they had now completely remodelled the constitution of the Football Association. In its present constitution they would not know it as the institution it was fifteen years ago. It was now nearly as democratic a republic as it was possible to make it".

"The Football Association comprised and governed the whole of England, but they could quite understand that a number of gentlemen who met in London could not govern so wide a space of country. They were not paid for it, and had no special interest in it except a love of the sport, and therefore they could not expect them, even if they could, to thoroughly govern the whole of the associations and clubs in the country. He and several of his friends had long considered that the country ought to be divided into districts, but they found some little difficulty in carrying that out through some of the counties who had football associations of their own not liking to be interfered with".

"But the idea was [accepted] that the Football Association should govern the whole of the country through affiliated associations, and that each association should have a distinct and definite section of the country allotted to it. Thus all the associations were directly representative of the association in London, and were responsible for the proper governing of the clubs in their districts. The Birmingham Association [for example] had allotted to it a radius of 35 miles round the city, and they were also responsible for the counties of Gloucestershire, Worcestershire, and Herefordshire. Local associations were being formed for each of these counties, and these would be responsible to Birmingham for the good conduct of their clubs. If a club was affiliated with [a local] Association, that association was affiliated with the Birmingham Association, and through that body the club was a direct member of the Football Association, and amenable to the rules. That club therefore, if it liked, could send a representative to Birmingham who would be entitled to a direct voice in the management of the association of that city. What they wanted the clubs to feel was that, though they were split up in sections, they were part and parcel of one whole, who had one object, and that to govern football all over England".

Of historical interest is that during his speech Campbell Orr referred to the "*Affiliation Rule*" which would come into force just over a month later on 1 November 1893. He was keen to stress that this rule, under which each club must be affiliated to a local Association affiliated to a County Association, "*did not imply that every schoolboy who played football, or school team, should be affiliated with an Association, but it applied to every club worthy of the name. It was not a rule forcing clubs to join any particular Association. If they did not like to belong to [a particular] Association they could belong to any other Association in their district, but they must be responsible to some Association for the conduct of their respective clubs*".

# Chapter 11: Campbell Orr on conduct of players and the game

Having spoken about the Association Football rules and organisation, Campbell Orr turned his attention to the matters of conduct of players, teamwork, and the roles of individual players on the field. His own extensive expertise, from over 20 years as a player and referee, comes through clearly in his references to the qualities required of the players.

**Conduct of players** - he explained that the Football Association "felt that it was not always what it ought to be ... and that it must be kept under control. They also felt that it could not be kept under control by individual clubs, but only by the local Association". The Football Association's position was that "If you turn your football field into a bear garden, we will stop you playing football". The intention was, he said, "to keep all ruffianism and brutality out of the game". However, he also pointed out that if a local Association dealt with a club harder than the club thought was just, then that club could appeal to the County Association and even to the Football Association in London.

**Teamwork** – "A player in the first place must be perfectly unselfish. A selfish player was no use to himself or his club. He might raise the cheers of the crowd, but he would never win a match; he might score a goal occasionally but he would be of no real use to a club. But a player must avoid the other extreme, for there was a danger of being too unselfish. He had seen in matches far too much unselfishness; by far too much passing. A team should play as a whole; each man should do his part, but that part unselfishly".

**Captaincy** – "A team of captains, like too many cooks, would not work well together at all. They ought to have one captain, and one only. If they were all ordering one another about they would not come off victorious often. Whilst they were quarrelling their opponents would be scoring goals, and the goals counted and the other did not. A captain should be a player somewhat superior to the rest in the team, and a person who could command respect and be looked up to. Whatever he said should be law, for that was the only way to bring out a successful team".

**Forwards** – "ought always to work and work hard. There was no good in any forward lying out just on the border line waiting for the ball to come to him, but he must work from the beginning of the game until the end of it. He had no patience with a player who came off the field fresh after playing for an hour and a half, and they could depend upon it that that man had not been really playing his best. He liked to see every forward in a team go away both up the right and left wings, and depend upon it nothing discomposed their opponents so much as to see the whole string of forwards going well up the field together. If the ball was going up the right wing [then] the left wing and centre should go up also".

**Half-backs** – "they should be the best men they could get, for they had the hardest work to do; they had to attack as well as defend. They had to help the forwards, and they could considerably help them provided they marked their distance. They should not be too close up, for if they were the ball would be sent over their heads, and if they were too far back they would lose many chances of attack".

**Backs** - he thought that "they should be the fastest men in the team, but he knew his opinion was not shared by all his football friends. Too much space should not be allowed between the half-backs and the backs, because if this were so, and the half-backs could not rely on the exact position of the backs, their efforts to pass them the ball and bring relief would be futile. It was a most dangerous thing to pass to the backs unless they could be thoroughly depended upon".

**The goalkeeper** – "should be a sturdy athlete, smart with his hands, and able to get the ball away without the slightest hesitation. If he hesitated he was lost. If he was a cricketer, and had been accustomed to keep wicket, so much the better".

**Composure** – "All players must keep their temper; the player who lost his temper lost his head, and then things generally went wrong. He had never known a man able to give an intelligent account of a game in which he had played if he had lost his temper".

He then covered the vexed subject of "*charging*" which, although within the laws, could give cause to injury. His view was that "charging ought to be avoided", and "his expertise, both theoretical and practical, was that it was far better to avoid a charge than take one. They should also remember that the man who was fond of charging got eleven bumps whilst his opponents would only get one".

Campbell Orr concluded his speech by covering the valuable role that the Football Association was playing in raising funds for charitable causes.

At the end of the speech questions were invited from the audience. A Mr Sutton asked the first one – on the "*Offside Rule*". Nothing changes!

## Chapter 12: Birmingham v Scotland – *"The Junior Internationals"*

Campbell Orr oversaw the growth of clubs playing the game at all levels. It is clear that he saw the development of the grass roots of the game as being as important as the rapid strides made by the major clubs like Aston Villa. His interest in the development of the game led him to have discussions with William Reid, the Secretary of the Scottish Junior Football Association (SJFA), to establish matches between representative junior sides drawn from the clubs within the Birmingham and Scottish Associations. The SJFA was also eager to test their skills against other sides, and Birmingham was seen to be drawing from a similar-sized club and player base as the SJFA with players of the same standard.

The fixtures which Campbell Orr and William Reid organised between a Birmingham FA junior team and the SJFA commenced in 1894, and quickly became dubbed *"The Junior Internationals"*. They were to continue for nearly 60 years until the start of the Second World War.

Prior to 1894 the Birmingham Association had already played a series of matches against a Scottish Counties team. Spectator numbers record the growing popularity of these fixtures. The first match on 18 January 1879 resulted in a 7-1 win for the Scots at Hampden Park, Glasgow, watched by 400 spectators. Birmingham hosted the Scottish Counties at the Lower Grounds, Aston, on 17 January 1880 and narrowly lost 2-3 in front of a crowd of 8,000. The venue returned to Glasgow on 19 February 1881 at Cathkin Park, with the Scots victorious in a 6-0 win watched by 3,000. On 25 February 1882 Birmingham won their first match 3-1 again at Aston Lower Grounds, with Vaughton, Holden and Woodcock scoring the goals in front of a crowd said to have been between 10,000 and 15,000. The last of these matches against Scottish Counties was played at Powderhall, Edinburgh, on 27 January 1883 where honours were even at 2-2 (crowd size not known at the time of writing).

**The opening of The Hawthorns on 3 September 1900**

Campbell Orr is at the rear and the first on the left with a bowler hat.

West Bromwich Albion players and officials together with other dignitaries at the first match at their new ground, versus Derby County.

*Back row*: I. Whitehouse (President, B'ham League), W. Heath (Sec. Staffs FA), J. C. Orr (Sec. B'ham F.A.), Dr. I. Pitt (Director), T. H. Sidney (Vice-President, Football League), H. Lockett (Sec. Football League).

*Third row*: H. Powell (Director), T. Harris Spencer (Director), H. Radford (Football League), C. E. Sutcliffe (Football League), D. Haigh (Vice-President, Football League), J. J. Bentley (President, Football League), H. Keys (Chairman of Directors), W. W. Hart (Football League), W. McGregor (Founder, Football League), C. Perry (Director), J. Lones (Director).

*Second row*: Frank Heaven (Sec.), Clement Keys (Auditor), T. Pickering, F. Wheldon (Captain), C. Simmons, A. Jones, A. Dunn, A. Adams, Jack Paddock (trainer).

*First row*: J. M. Bayliss (Director), J. Chadburn, R. J. Roberts, J. Reader, W. Williams, H. Hadley.

With regard to *"The Junior Internationals"* from 1894 onwards, Campbell Orr realised the need to ensure that these were competitive matches, but at the outset this was hampered by Birmingham and the SJFA having different organisational structures and team selection criteria. The Birmingham Football Association membership embraced all clubs in the area and of all standards, but initially the Birmingham "junior" team was selected only from players in those clubs which were not in the Football League. This gave the Scots an advantage, in that the majority of talented Scottish junior players were within the SJFA and available for selection, whereas many talented Birmingham junior players within the Football League clubs were excluded. This anomaly was apparent in the match results. Therefore Birmingham's selection rules were changed so that a player from any club could be selected provided that the player himself had not played in a Football League or FA Cup game. Campbell Orr understood that Birmingham's next generation of top players would be found from those currently playing in the reserve teams of his Birmingham FA Football League member clubs, while in Scotland it was the top Junior clubs which already provided a conveyor belt of talent to the top Scottish clubs. This understanding of the different arrangements North and South of the Border resulted in the annual *"Junior International"* fixture becoming compulsory viewing for English and Scottish League clubs looking for new talent.

Taking a team from Birmingham to Scotland involved significant costs, not least the travelling, and Campbell Orr was concerned to ensure that these costs were adequately financed. He realised that the fixtures played in Scotland drew bigger crowds and larger gate receipts than the games played in Birmingham. At the turn of the century the games played in Glasgow were drawing gate receipts of around £300, compared with only around £45 for the games played in Birmingham. Therefore in 1901 Campbell Orr negotiated a guarantee of a contribution for Birmingham of £25 from the gate receipts for the matches in Glasgow. Then in 1906 he secured an increased guarantee of a £50 contribution, despite this leading to the threat of a boycott of the fixture by the SJFA. In response Campbell Orr pointed out that the Football Association would not sanction the Scots playing any other English representative team for this fixture, and hence it was in the Scots' best interest to agree to the contribution.

Whilst *"The Junior Internationals"* were organised by Campbell Orr under the auspices of the Birmingham Association, it seems that the Council of the Association as a whole may have had misgivings with regard to the fixture being called *"The Junior International"* and the Birmingham team being dubbed *"England"*, at least in the publicity North of the Border. These terms were known to be misnomers, but Campbell Orr used his political skills to smooth this over. As a Scot with a commercial mind he clearly understood that billing the game in Glasgow as *"The Junior International – Scotland v England"* was the very reason for the excellent gate receipts from which he had secured the contribution guarantees. In the end it was agreed that *"so long as the Birmingham Association are not a party to the misnomer no great harm is done whatever the fixture is styled"*.

Many great players made their first representative appearances in *"The Junior International"*, and then went on to play for their respective countries at full international level. Amongst the players who progressed to play League football was Leslie Crump, the great nephew of another *"Grand Old Man of Midland Football"* Charles Crump, who played in the 1925 match at The Hawthorns, West Bromwich. The longevity of this fixture from 1894 to 1939, with a brief resumption from 1972 to 1976, is testimony to Campbell Orr's work in establishing the administrative arrangements between the two Associations.

Whilst Campbell Orr was for the most part involved with the matches against Scotland, it is known that other fixtures were organised against Irish and Welsh junior representative teams. Indeed a few years earlier Campbell Orr himself played centre forward for Birmingham in their 0-1 defeat by a team representing North Wales played on 10 February 1877 at Wrexham. The team was captained by George Ramsay of Aston Villa Football Club, who went on to be the most successful secretary-manager in Villa's history.

# Chapter 13: Campbell Orr Shield and Campbell Orr Memorial Trophy

In keeping with Campbell Orr's personal interest in the development of the junior game, two junior competitions bore his name – the "Campbell Orr Shield" and the "Campbell Orr Memorial Trophy". The former commenced within his lifetime and the latter, as the name implies, commenced after his death.

Although he came from a commercial background, Campbell Orr was initially an opponent of professionalism in the sport, and he used his newspaper column to campaign against it. With clubs in Lancashire starting to engage professionals, he was keen that this should not begin in the Midlands. As he saw it he felt that professionalism would damage the game as a sport, and as a former player he simply wanted players to enjoy the game and the friendships as much as he had. In his view professionalism was a threat to this ideal, which perhaps explains why he did so much to develop the junior and amateur game in Birmingham.

The Campbell Orr Shield, donated for competition by Campbell Orr himself shortly before his death, was competed for between teams made up of the best players representing local amateur leagues in the Birmingham FA area. He wanted the best footballers to have the opportunity to play against one another over and above the normal inter-club matches. Early newspaper coverage simply called the competition *"the knock-out competition for local leagues promoted by the Birmingham FA"*, although later on it was widely reported as the Campbell Orr Shield. Indeed Campbell Orr's motive in establishing the competition was deeper. The first competition early in 1921 was used by the Birmingham FA selectors to watch the top local players in action against one another, in order to help them to select the team to play Junior Scotland in the annual fixture at Villa Park on 9 April 1921. While the selectors would know the players in the Birmingham League and Birmingham Combination competitions, they also wanted to watch other good players in the area.

Sixteen local leagues entered the first Campbell Orr Shield competition, and the first round was played on 12 February 1921. The first final was played at Leamington on 7 May 1921 when the Coventry and North Warwickshire League defeated the Trent Valley League 4-0. Apart from the years of the Second World War the Campbell Orr Shield was competed for continuously until the Birmingham and District Amateur FA won the last competition in 1994/95. The Birmingham Football Association records simply state *"1995 onwards – not competed for"*. Research of the post-war years reveals that the annual final was often played at Villa Park or St Andrews, which signifies that this was considered to be an important competition.

Much less is known about the Campbell Orr Memorial Trophy, other than that it was competed for by works sides. Football Annuals covering 1948/49 to 1966/67 record the competition, but at the time of writing it has not been possible to establish when the competition started or finished. The word "Memorial" in the title suggests that the competition may have started in the years immediately after Campbell Orr's death, and that the trophy may have been donated by his many football friends and colleagues or perhaps his family.

It is also not known at the time of writing whether either the Shield or Trophy are still in existence. The authors would welcome information regarding these, or any other information with regard to the life and achievements of Campbell Orr.

# Chapter 14: Family life in Birmingham

From the time of his arrival in Birmingham Campbell Orr was a merchant's clerk and worked for the Birmingham merchants, J C & W Lord. He lived for a time in Wheeler Street, Birmingham. He married Ellen Elizabeth Marsh on Christmas Day 1880 and they lived in Bull Street, Harborne.

The couple had a family of five sons and two daughters. The family lived in St Peters Road, Handsworth, and later City Road, Edgbaston. Alongside his family, work and football life he was a leading member of the Scottish community and for a time was President of the Midlands Scottish Society.

**Family photograph taken at the family home at 23 City Road, Birmingham circa 1910**
Standing from left to right: Kenneth (son), Andrew (son), Campbell Orr, Graeme (son), Marjorie (daughter).
Sitting from left to right: Norman (son), Ellen (wife), Wilhelmina (daughter), Gordon (son).

# Chapter 15: His final years

Campbell Orr continued his active involvement as Secretary of the Birmingham County Football Association into his 70's. His wife Ellen died in April 1921 and by all accounts he flung himself into his work as a way of dealing with his grief. On 10 November, days after attending the Aston Villa v Middlesbrough match on 29 October, a 6-2 win for Villa in front of a crowd of 30,000, he caught influenza that in the end proved fatal. Campbell Orr died on 16 November 1921, just under a month after his 71st birthday.

A memorial service was held on 18 November 1921 at Christ Church, Summerfield, Birmingham followed by interment in the churchyard of St Peter's Church in Harborne. At the service the family was joined by the world of football. This included representatives of the Birmingham FA, the senior clubs and the local leagues around the city:

**Birmingham County FA**

Mr Charles Crump, President (Senior Vice President, Football Association)

Mr Walter W Hart, Chairman

Mr John Adams, Treasurer

**Staffordshire FA**

Mr Harry Keys, President

**Walsall FA**

Mr Ebenezer Smith

**Worcestershire FA**

Mr Charles Austin, Chairman

Mr A Hope, Secretary

Lt Col William H Carter DSO MC

**Coventry FA**

Mr W J Harris

**Birmingham Works FA**

Mr John H Webster

Mr J Grayson

**Birmingham Youths' and Old Boys' FA**

Mr Frank H Ward

**West Bromwich Charity FA**

Mr T J Morris

**Aston Villa FC**

Mr Frederick W Rinder, Chairman

Mr Walker Strange, Assistant Secretary

**Birmingham FC**

Mr Thomas W Turley, Director

Mr Frank W Richards, Manager

**West Bromwich Albion FC**

Mr Frederick Everiss, Secretary-Manager

**Wolverhampton Wanderers FC**

Mr Henry Dallard

**National Association of Referees and Birmingham Combination**

Mr Ernest Spiers

**Birmingham Combination**

Mr Joseph Tillotson, President

**Victoria League**

Mr L W Salt

**Sparkbrook League**

Mr W A Hollins

**Handsworth and Smethwick Leagues**

Representatives not named

**Birmingham Alliance**

Mr E Jennings

**Also attending**

Mr Louis Ford of Walsall, a former Vice-President of the Birmingham FA, FA Councillor, Vice President of the Football League and director of West Bromwich Albion

The location of Campbell Orr's grave within St Peter's churchyard has not been identified by the authors at the time of writing, despite several visits to the churchyard and Parish Office. It is understood that the relevant records were destroyed by a fire at the church in 1972. For anyone willing to pursue the quest, it is believed that the grave of John Campbell Orr and his wife Ellen is not in the part of the churchyard used for interments in 1921 when they died. The grave is more likely to be in the area used in 1885, as Campbell and Ellen had an eighth child, George, who died in infancy in that year, and it is understood that they were buried in the same grave.

# Chapter 16: His legacy

Campbell Orr's legacy to Association Football in Birmingham is eloquently and completely recorded in a resolution passed by the Council of the Birmingham County Football Association at its meeting on 1 December 1921. This resolution was copied as an impressive illuminated scroll signed by the Council members, then framed and presented to the family of Campbell Orr as an expression of condolence and in appreciation and recognition of his work.

The original illuminated scroll, in a frame measuring 2ft 6ins tall by 2ft wide (760mm by 610mm), is still in the possession of the co-author of this book, Martin Shirley, a great grandson of Campbell Orr. The full text of the scroll appears overleaf on Page 40. The signatories were:

**Charles Crump**, President
**Walter W Hart**, Chairman
**John Adams**, Hon. Treasurer
**John Adams,** Referees Committee Chairman
**E Jennings**, Referees Committee Hon. Sec.
**Joseph C Tillotson JP**, Disciplinary Committee Chairman
**Thomas Robinson**, Disciplinary Committee Hon. Sec.
**Arthur J Selvage**, Benevolent Society Chairman
**Henry P Devey**, Benevolent Society Hon. Sec.
**Joseph S Round**, Match Committee Chairman
**Frank H Ward**, Match Committee Hon. Sec.
**Leonard Johnson**, League Sanction Committee Chairman
**Victor E Jones**, Finance Committee Chairman
**John Adams**, Gen. Sec. Pro. Tem.

## ***Birmingham County Football Association***

### ***Resolution passed at a Meeting of the Council held on December 1st, 1921:-***

*That the Officers and Members of the Council of the Birmingham County Football Association tender to the FAMILY OF MR. JOHN CAMPBELL ORR their deepest sympathy on the death of their Father, who was the devoted Secretary and Friend of the Association, the members of which truly share their sorrow and sincerely mourn his loss.*

*The Association with heartfelt gratitude and loving memories places on record that MR. JOHN CAMPBELL ORR as a player was amongst the first to introduce the game to Birmingham, and was one of the Founders of this Association in 1875.*

*He acted as the Honorary Secretary for the first two years of its formation, Hon. Treasurer for the next seven, and on the death of Mr. H. J. Cofield resumed the Secretaryship in 1884 [see footnote], retaining the Office until called to the "Great Beyond" November 16th, 1921. During that period the Association expanded from ten to over twelve hundred Clubs, bringing untold benefit to the physical well-being, recreation and enjoyment of the community, and raising of thousands of pounds for Charity, a success in a great measure due to Mr. Orr's able, devoted and enthusiastic labours.*

*He was a patient, unobtrusive, high minded manly man, of unfailing courtesy and tact, willing at all times to give others the benefit of his knowledge and experience, and by the example of his uprightness of character and Christian life, exercised considerable influence for good, which has been a predominant factor in the establishment of the game and its management on its present high-toned basis.*

Footnote: It is understood that the date of 1884 given as the year of the year of the death of Mr H J Cofield is an error and should read 1886.

# Birmingham County Football Association.

Resolution passed at a Meeting of the Council held on December 1st, 1921:-

"That the Officers and Members of the Council of the Birmingham County Football Association tender to the

## Family of Mr. John Campbell Orr

their deepest sympathy on the death of their Father, who was the devoted Secretary and Friend of the Association, the members of which truly share their sorrow and sincerely mourn his loss."

The Association with heartfelt gratitude and loving memories places on record that

## Mr. John Campbell Orr

as a player was amongst the first to introduce the game to Birmingham, and was one of the Founders of this Association in 1875.

He acted as the Honorary Secretary for the first two years of its formation, Hon. Treasurer for the next seven, and on the death of Mr. H. J. Cofield resumed the Secretaryship in 1884, retaining the office until called to the "Great Beyond" November 16th. 1921. During that period the Association expanded from ten to over twelve hundred Clubs, bringing untold benefit to the physical well-being, recreation and enjoyment of the community, and raising of thousands of pounds for Charity, a success in a great measure due to Mr. Orr's able, devoted and enthusiastic labours.

He was a patient, unobtrusive, high minded manly man, of unfailing courtesy and tact, willing at all times to give others the benefit of his knowledge and experience, and by the example of his uprightness of character and Christian life, exercised considerable influence for good, which has been a predominent factor in the establishment of the game and its management on its present high-toned basis."

Signed on behalf of the Council:-

President.

Walter W. Hart Chairman.

John Adams Hon. Treasurer.

Referees Committee. Chairman. / E. Jennings Hon. Sec.

Match Committee. Chairman. / Hon. Sec.

Disciplinary Committee. Chairman. / Hon. Sec.

League Sanct'n Committee. Chairman. / Hon. Sec.

Benevolent Society. Chairman. / H. P. Davey Hon. Sec.

Victor L. Jones Chairman Finance Committee.

John Adams Gen. Sec. Pro. Tem.

In addition to the words in the scroll, Campbell Orr's personal qualities are well illustrated in various quotations from the newspapers:

*"The dapper, quiet little figure, with the nimble tread, the keen mind, the alert eye, the genial disposition."* Sports Argus 19 November 1921

*"A hard-headed, a hard-thinking and a hard-working Scot."* Birmingham Mail circa 1910

*"A quiet, easy-going, unobtrusive typical Scotsman of the right sort – a cheery, even-tempered, far-seeing sportsman, and a living refutation of the calumny that anyone from "ayont the Tweed" cannot appreciate a joke."* Birmingham Mail circa 1910

*"Orr is recognised as one of the game's great administrators of the first fifty years."* newspaper cutting, unheaded

*"There is no more popular football official in the Kingdom than Mr Orr, who founded the first Association club in Birmingham and established the Birmingham and District Association."* Lancashire Evening Post - Tuesday 8 May 1900

*"He simply revels in routine and his application is boundless…….And if we can be pardoned the hackneyed phrase – what he does not know about football law and procedure is scarcely worth knowing"*. Birmingham Mail circa 1910

## References and Acknowledgements

Family records of the descendants of John Campbell Orr
"*Lost teams of the Midlands*" by Mike Bradbury published in 2013 ISBN 978-1-4836-9529-7
The British Newspaper Archive
The National Library of Scotland
"*Scotlandspeople*" website – National Records of Scotland
"*The Hawthorns Golden Jubilee – the story of West Bromwich Albion football ground 1900-1950*" by W. Ellery Jephcott 1950
All photographs and images, except one, are reproduced with kind permission of Martin Shirley.
The photograph from the opening of West Bromwich Albion's ground, The Hawthorns, was taken from a commemorative booklet "The Hawthorns Golden Jubilee – the story of West Bromwich Albion football ground 1900-1950" by W. Ellery Jephcott 1950.
Andy Mitchell – for advice and guidance
Scottishleague.net football forum members - for help with research
Robert Bradley – for help with research
Craig Pake – for advice and guidance
Image Centre Ltd, Bath – for assistance and advice with the reproduction of images, including digital repair
Scottish Football Historian – Edition 55 - "The Caledonian Quintet" by Hal Mason

www.ingramcontent.com/pod-product-compliance
Ingram Content Group UK Ltd.
Pitfield, Milton Keynes, MK11 3LW, UK
UKHW060111300726
14090UKWH00002B/132

* 9 7 8 1 5 2 7 2 0 4 7 2 0 *